# Earth

## Words by David Bennett
## Pictures by Rosalinda Kightley

A BANTAM LITTLE ROOSTER BOOK
™

**Toronto · New York · London · Sydney · Auckland**

We live on a planet called Earth. It is like
a big ball in space that travels around
and around the sun.

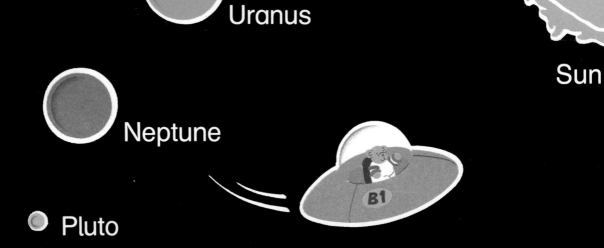

Saturn

Uranus

Neptune

Sun

Pluto

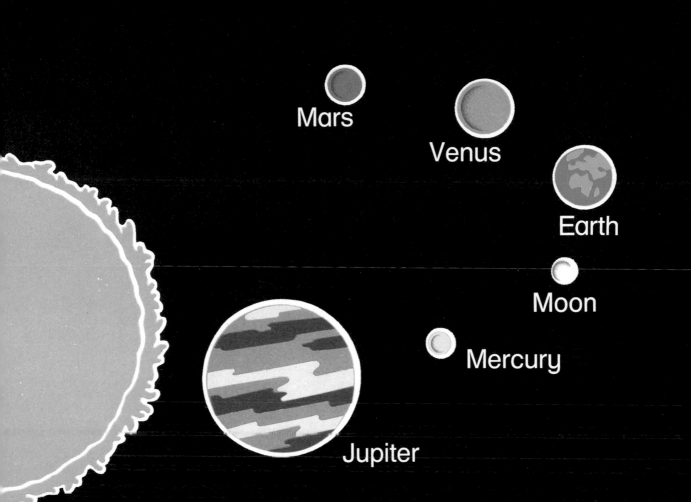

Mars

Venus

Earth

Moon

Mercury

Jupiter

There are eight other planets. Some are
bigger than earth and some are smaller.
Can you say their names? Remember,
the sun and the moon are not planets.

Thanks to air, water, and sunlight, our planet is filled with plants and animals.

Everyone on earth breathes air. It is part
of an invisible blanket called atmosphere.
Try to say *at-moss-fear.*

Over half the earth is covered by water.

The rest of the earth is covered by land.
It is split into pieces like a jigsaw puzzle.
These pieces are called continents.

As far as we know, earth is the only planet with life on it. That makes us special.

There is life in the water, on and under the ground, up in the trees, and in the sky.

The water we use comes from rivers, streams, and lakes. But most of the water on earth is found in the salty oceans.

Oceans are deep and full of mystery.
They are alive with plants of every color
and fish and sea animals of every size.

Around the middle of the earth, it is very hot and rains almost every day. This part of the earth is called the equator.

Great jungles full of giant trees grow there.
Brightly colored parrots screech as
monkeys swing through the treetops.

Unlike the equator, the top and bottom of the earth are very cold places. We call them the poles. Thick ice covers the land and floats in the water.

Only a few plants and animals are able to live at the poles. A polar bear has thick fur that keeps out the freezing cold weather.

Deserts are some of the driest places on earth.
It is difficult to find water because it almost
never rains. But there are some plants and
animals in the deserts.

A palm tree has long roots to search for
water deep under the ground.

A camel stores fat in its hump. When it is hungry or thirsty, it turns the fat into food.

People live all around the world.

Some people live in big cities and some in small towns. Other people live in the country or near the water.

If we could slice open the earth, it would look a little like an apple.

The land and water are like the skin of the apple. And the middle of the earth is like the apple's core. Underneath the land and water the rock is so hot it melts.

The earth is millions and millions of years old. It is changing all the time. Mountains are formed when pieces of land move together.

Over time, wind and rain wear down the mountains. These things happen very slowly.

Not all changes happen slowly.
An earthquake is sudden. In an earthquake,
the ground shakes — so do trees
and buildings.

Volcanoes can be found where the earth's skin has cracked open. Melted rock called lava shoots out of some volcanoes.

We have also found ways to make changes of our own.

We have learned many things by studying the earth.
But if we want our planet to last a million more years,
we have to learn how to take care of it.

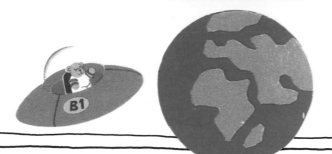

# BEAR REVIEW

1. We live on a Planet called Earth.
   It travels around and around the sun.

2. The land on earth is split into pieces
   called continents. But over half of the
   earth is covered by water.

3. The earth is warmest around the middle
   of the planet and coldest at the top and
   bottom. What are these places called?

4. The Earth is very old, but it is still
   changing.